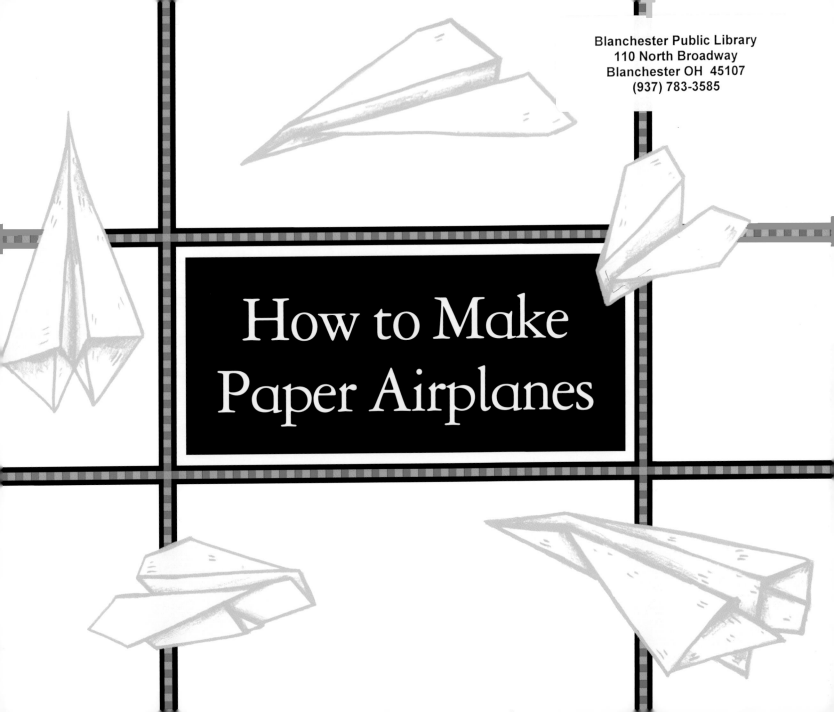

How to Make Paper Airplanes

The Child's World

Published by The Child's World®
1980 Lookout Drive • Mankato, MN 56003-1705
800-599-READ • www.childsworld.com

Acknowledgments
The Child's World®: Mary Berendes, Publishing Director
Red Line Editorial: Editorial direction and production
The Design Lab: Design

Photographs ©: Mark Yuill/Shutterstock Images, 4

ISBN: 978-1623235628
LCCN: 2013931424

Printed in the United States of America
Mankato, MN
July, 2013
PA02176

ABOUT THE AUTHOR

B. B. Adams writes trivia, humor, and fiction in books and on the Internet. He lives in Oregon with his family.

ABOUT THE ILLUSTRATOR

Kelsey Oseid is an illustrator and graphic designer from Minneapolis, Minnesota. When she's not drawing, she likes to do craft projects, bake cookies, go on walks, and play with her two cats, Jamie and Fiona. You can find her work at www.kelseyoseid.com.

Table of Contents

Amazing Paper

Flat paper doesn't fly. Hold up a piece of printer paper. Then let it go. It slowly drifts to the ground. Boring! But try folding this same piece of paper. You can make it fly, swoop, and soar through the air! Making paper airplanes is easy to do. All you need is a piece of paper.

Have fun flying these six paper airplanes. Learn what works and what does not work. Soon you'll be able to design your own planes!

For the projects in this book you'll need:

- 6 sheets of printer paper
- Scissors
- Tape

The Arrow

The arrow is the first paper airplane most people ever make.

STEP
2

1 Fold the sheet of paper in half the long way. Now the paper should be shaped a little like a hot dog bun. Then open up the folded paper. Hold it like an open book.

2 Fold one of the top corners in toward the center crease. Then fold the other top corner down to the center crease.

3 Start at the point. Fold the angled edge of each side of the paper down toward the center crease. The inside edges should line up with the center crease.

4 Turn the plane over. Now fold the plane in half along the center crease.

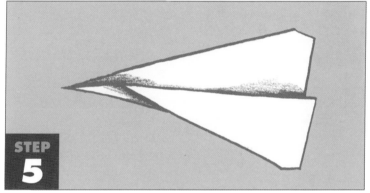

5 Fold the first wing down partway. The edge of the fold should end about 1 inch (2.5 cm) from the center.

6 Repeat **step 5** with the other wing.

Now just hold the plane in the middle and throw!

The Dart

The dart is another easy airplane to make.

STEP 1

STEP 3

1 Start out by folding the paper in half the wide way. Then unfold the paper.

2 Fold the top two corners in toward the center.

3 Fold the edges of the paper again. The edges should line up with the center crease.

STEP 5

STEP 7

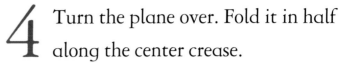 Turn the plane over. Fold it in half along the center crease.

5 Fold the first wing down to about 1 inch (2.5 cm) from the center crease of the plane.

6 Repeat **step 5** on the other side.

7 Put a small piece of tape just under the wings at the rear of the plane. Now let it fly!

The Flying Fish

WHAT YOU'LL NEED:
- 1 piece of printer paper
- Scissors

This airplane is a little different. Pay attention when you are flying it. How does it fly differently than the last two planes you made? How might the design change the way the plane flies?

STEP 1

1 To start out, carefully cut a strip from the long side of the paper. The strip should be about 1 inch (2.5 cm) wide. You will use this strip to make your plane!

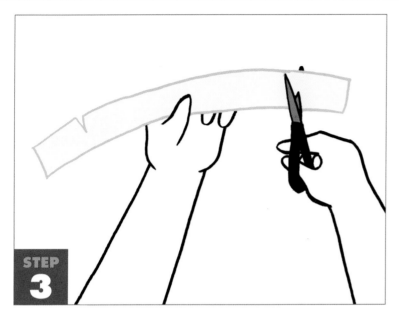

STEP 3

STEP 6

2   Find the left edge of the strip. Cut a small notch about 2 inches (5 cm) from the top.

3   Find the right edge of the strip. Cut another notch about 2 inches (5 cm) up from the bottom.

4   Pull the two ends of the paper together. This makes a circle.

5   Now just slip the notches into each other. It will look like a fish!

6   Finally it's time to toss your fish in the air.

Watch it spin as it falls to the ground!

The Nakamura Lock

This paper airplane is based on the Japanese paper-folding art called **origami**.

STEP
3

1 First fold the paper in half the long way. Unfold the paper.

2 Fold the top corners down to the center crease.

3 Now fold the whole top triangle down onto the rest of the paper. The tip of the triangle should line up with the center crease.

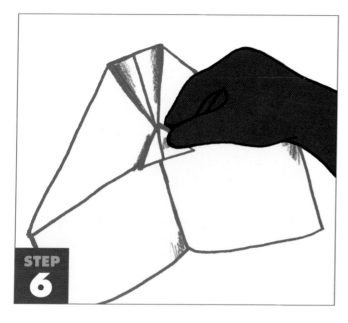

4 Fold about 1 inch (2.5 cm) of the tip of the triangle up. Now unfold it back down.

5 Fold the top corners down to the center. The corners should meet just above the crease you made when you folded the tip in **step** 4.

6 Fold the tip up. It should cover the corners you folded down in **step** 5.

7 Now turn the plane over. Then fold the plane in half.

8 Fold down each of the wings to about 1 inch (2.5 cm) from the center crease.

Now your plane is ready for flight!

Great Glider

A **glider** is a plane that can sail for a long distance. Follow these steps to make this simple and swift glider.

1 Begin by folding the paper in half the wide way. Now unfold the paper.

2 Fold down each of the top corners. The corners should meet on the center crease. You should have a triangle on top of the plane.

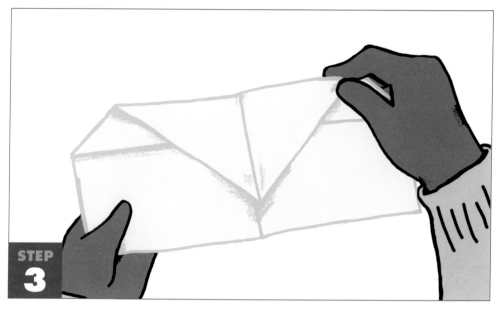

3 Fold the tip of the triangle down to about 1 inch (2.5 cm) from the edge of the paper.

4 Next fold the top edge of the paper down about 1 inch (2.5 cm).

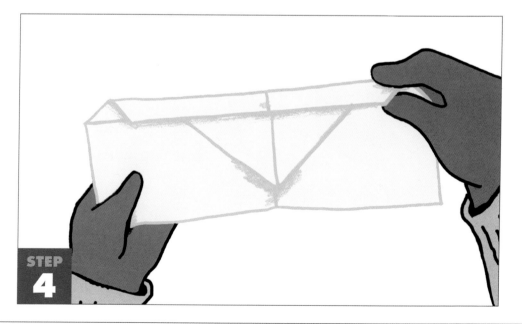

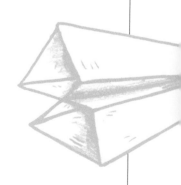

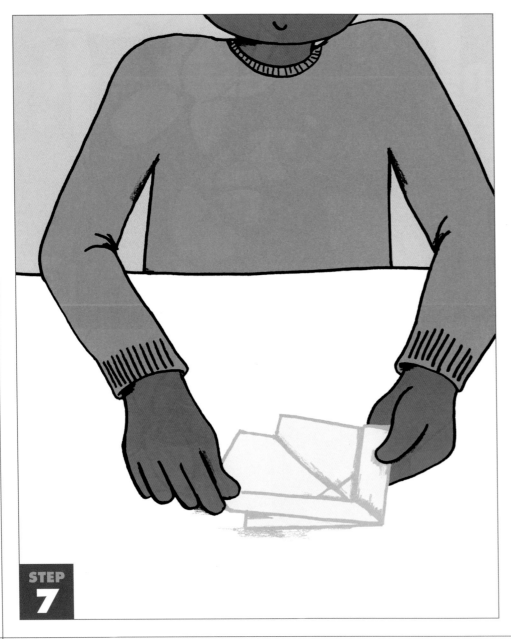

5 Now fold the plane in half along the center crease. None of your folds should be showing.

6 Lay the plane on the table so the corner without a point is on the bottom right.

7 Fold up the bottom edge of the plane so it lines up with the left edge. You have made your first wing!

STEP
7

STEP
9

KEEP A FLIGHT LOG
Keep track of how far each of your planes flies. Make sure to stand in the same place each time. Measure the distance to the spot where each plane lands. Which plane flies the farthest? Think about what parts of each plane's design help it fly far. Write this information down. You can use this **data** to make improvements the next time you make paper airplanes.

8 Repeat **step 7** on the other side.

9 Now just put a small piece of tape on the bottom of the plane. This will keep the wings from coming apart.

WHAT YOU'LL NEED:

- 1 piece of printer paper
- Scissors

The Remnant

A **remnant** is something that is left over. This plane uses less than a whole sheet of paper. It also requires some careful cutting. This little plane can fly far!

STEP
2

1 Take your piece of paper. Fold down the top right corner so the top edge of the paper lines up with the left side.

2 The fold will make a rectangle of paper at the bottom. Cut off

18

the rectangle part. This is the remnant. This is what you will make the plane from.

3 Fold the top left corner down to the bottom right corner.

4 Rotate the plane so the crease you made is on top. Fold this top part down about ½ inch (1.2 cm).

STEP
4

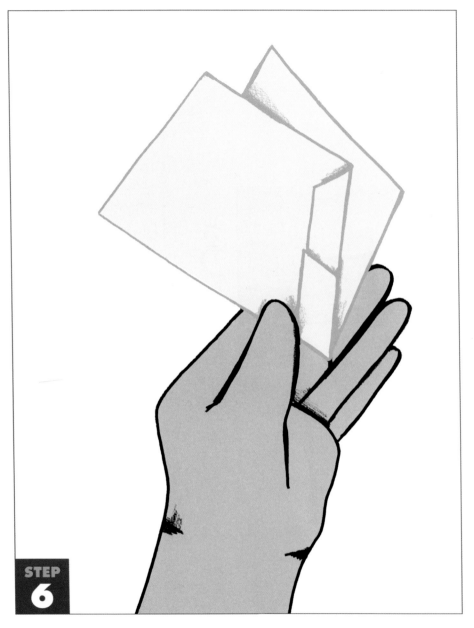

5 Repeat **step** 4 two more times.

6 Fold the plane in half so the folds you made in **steps** 4 and 5 are on the outside.

7 Next fold the wing flaps down. The edge of each wing should line up with the center crease.

Now just give it a throw!

STEP
7

Glossary

crease (KREES): A crease is the fold in something, such as paper. Running your fingernail or a coin over a crease will help your paper airplane stay together.

data (DAY-tuh): Data is information collected for a specific use. Using the data gathered from your paper airplane flights can help improve a paper airplane's design.

glider (GLYE-dur): A glider is a lightweight airplane designed to fly far with no engine power. Your glider should travel a long distance.

gravity (GRAV-i-tee): Gravity is the force that pulls objects toward the earth. Paper airplanes must overcome gravity to fly.

lift (LIFT): Lift is the force that works against the weight of an object and holds it in the air. Lift helps paper airplanes fly.

origami (or-i-GAH-mee): Origami is the Japanese art of paper folding. The Nakamura lock paper airplane design is based on origami.

remnant (REM-nuhnt): A remnant is a leftover small amount of something. You can use the remnant of a full piece of paper to make a small paper airplane.

Learn More

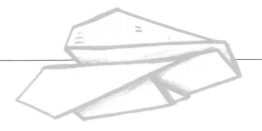

Books

Dewar, Andrew. *Fun and Easy Paper Airplanes*. North Clarendon, VT: Tuttle, 2008.

Robinson, Nick. *Making Paper Airplanes: That Really Fly*. New York: Sterling, 2004.

Schmidt, Norman. *Best Ever Paper Airplanes*. New York: Sterling, 2007.

Web Sites

Visit our Web site for links about making paper airplanes: *childsworld.com/links*

Note to Parents, Teachers, and Librarians: We routinely verify our Web links to make sure they are safe and active sites. So encourage your readers to check them out!

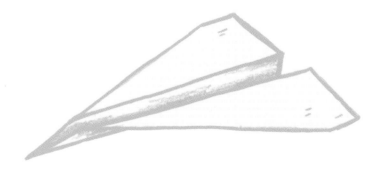

Index

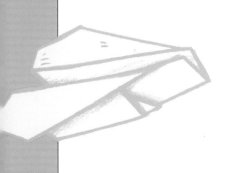